MT.
GW00937962

Life in Early Times

 Colourpoint

Dedicated to the memory of
Dr Austin Logan, whose vision
and energy inspired this project.

All rights reserved. No part of this publication
may be reproduced, stored in a retrieval system,
or transmitted in any form by any means,
electronic, mechanical, photocopying, recording
or otherwise, without the prior written
permission of the copyright owner and
publisher of this book.

ISBN 1 898392 23 4

8 7 6 5 4 3 2

© The Education and Library
Boards of N. Ireland
1996

Acknowledgments

Images Colour Library	56 (pyramids).
Ulster Museum	13 (harpoon and microliths); 34 (axeheads); 43; 45.
Mary Evans Picture Lib.	6; 55; 56 (lower); 57 (tomb).
The Dept. of Arts, Culture and the Gaeltacht, Ireland	53; 54 (top).
Dept of the Environment for N. Ireland	12; 14.
Norman Johnston	7; 13 (top); 37 (bottom two).
Ulster History Park	15; 20; 34; 36; 37 (top); 44; 47 (bottom); 48 (bottom); 49 (bottom).
Anthony Candon	47 (top); 48 (top); 49 (top); 50; 52; 54.

Written, revised and edited by:	Austin Logan, Sheila Tinsley, Rhonda Glasgow, Vivien Kelly, Maurice Todd.
Illustrators:	Gerry Bradley, John Brogan.
Layout and design:	Sheila Johnston

Colourpoint Books
Unit D5 Ards Business Centre
Jubilee Road
NEWTOWNARDS
Co Down
BT23 4YH

Tel: (028) 9182 0505
Fax: (028) 9182 1900
E-mail: info@colourpoint.co.uk
Web site: www.colourpoint.co.uk

The publisher and editors of this book would like to
record their appreciation of the generous help given
during its compilation by Anthony Candon, director of
the Ulster History Park at Omagh; by Greer Ramsay of
Armagh County Museum; and by the Archaeology and
Ethnography Department, and the Education
Department at the Ulster Museum in Belfast. Their
comments and guidance have been invaluable.
Thanks also to the many teachers, advisers and
inspectors, north and south, who participated in the
conference held at Slane in July 1993, and whose
contributions provided the impetus for this project.

Contents

Your long journey back in time!

This is a story of Ireland long, long ago.

It starts with the first people who lived by hunting and gathering and shows how that way of life changed after the first farmers arrived.

Timeline

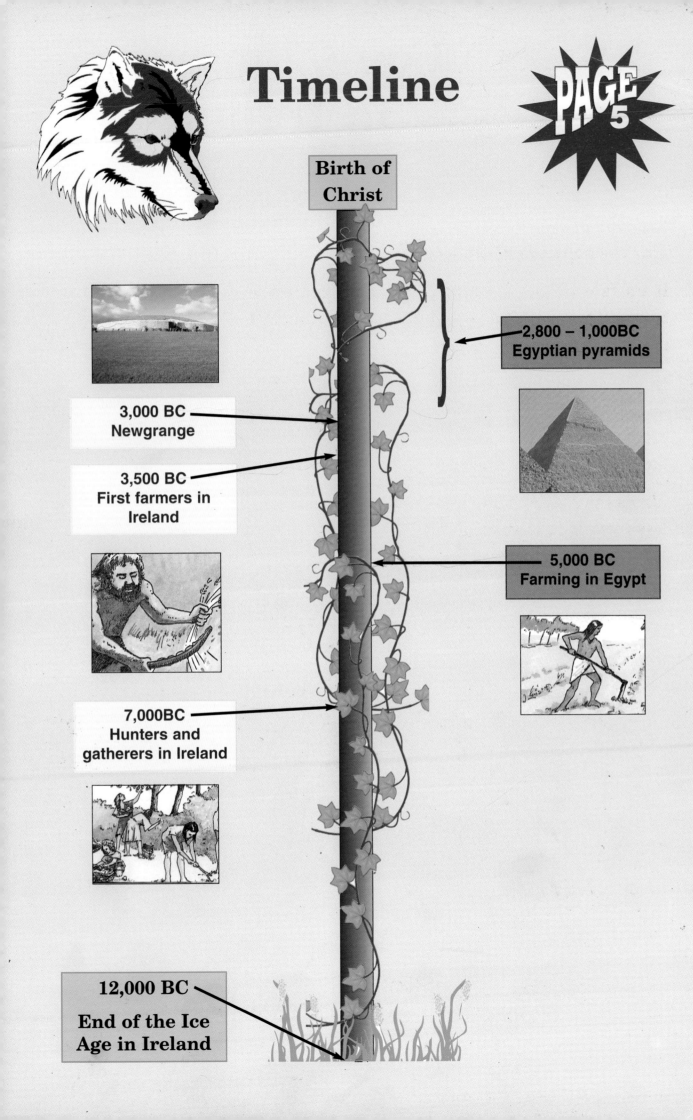

Birth of Christ

2,800 – 1,000BC Egyptian pyramids

3,000 BC Newgrange

3,500 BC First farmers in Ireland

5,000 BC Farming in Egypt

7,000BC Hunters and gatherers in Ireland

12,000 BC End of the Ice Age in Ireland

Long, long ago in Ireland

Long, long, long ago, Ireland was a very cold place.

It was much colder than it is today.

It was so cold that no living thing could live in Ireland.

It was the Ice Age and most of Ireland was covered in ice and snow.

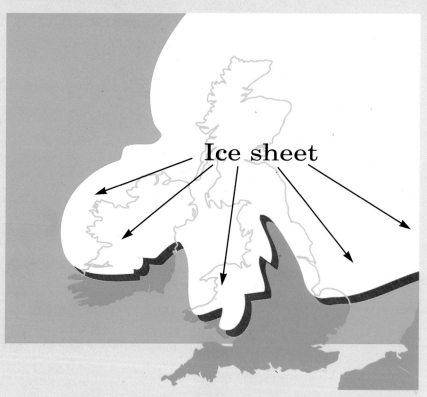

Ice sheet

About 20,000 years ago, ice sheets covered most of the British Isles.

No rain fell, only snow, and it stayed on the land so the sea level went down.

Ireland after the Ice Age

Gradually the climate got warmer and the ice began to melt.

The Ice Age was over.

Ireland became a land of lakes and forests. As time went by, animals spread to Ireland from the east and south.

Then the first people came to Ireland. They had to cross the sea to get there.

Much of Ireland looked like this after the Ice Age.

The Irish Sea was not always as wide as it is today. Long, long ago, when the first people came to Ireland, the sea was much narrower.

The orange areas on this map show you where the coastline was at that time.

The green areas show you the coastline as we know it today.

Ireland

Irish Sea

Britain

The first people come to Ireland

Perhaps the first people came to Ireland in boats like this one.

This boat is made from animal skins stretched over a frame made of branches.

Talk about how a boat like this was made.

What do you think it would have been like to cross the sea in this boat?

How would it be moved?

How would you steer it?

What would the people need to bring with them?

Hunters and gatherers

The first people in Ireland lived in a very different way from the way we do today.

They could not buy their food from shops and supermarkets like we do.

Instead they had to hunt for their food, or gather it from the bushes and trees. They were **hunters** and **gatherers**.

Because they used stone tools and weapons, we call this time the **Stone Age**. The first people to come to Ireland were **Mesolithic** or **Middle Stone Age** people.

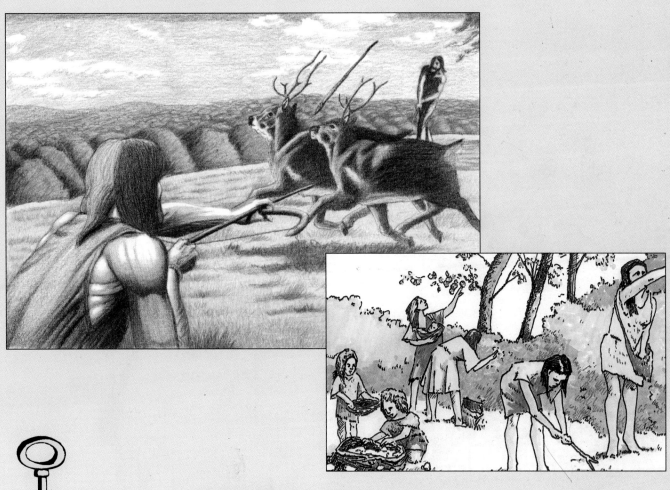

hunter, gatherer, Mesolithic, Middle Stone Age.

The larder

On the opposite page is a picture of the kind of countryside that people lived in. The river is flowing out into the sea.

Here are some of the animals and plants that the Mesolithic people would have hunted and gathered for food. Say where you think each of them would be found.

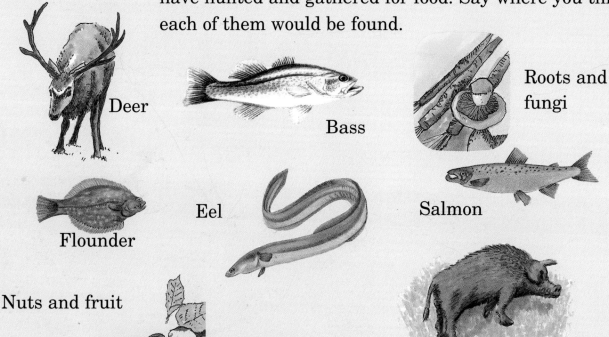

Deer

Bass

Roots and fungi

Flounder

Eel

Salmon

Nuts and fruit

Wild Boar

Here are some useful facts

Flounder and bass are sea fish.
Salmon live in the sea and the rivers.

In spring and summer salmon leave the sea and swim up the rivers to spawn.

In autumn, eels leave the river and head for the sea to spawn.

In autumn, groups of wild boar roam the woodlands searching for nuts, fruit and fungi.

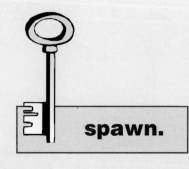

spawn.

How do we know?

Mesolithic people lived a very long time ago, before books were written, so how do we know about them?

Most of the **evidence** comes from **artefacts** and other **clues** hidden under the ground.

People who search for evidence of the past are called **archaeologists**.

Here are some archaeologists at work.

Here are some things which you might see if you were able to dig down through the ground near your house.

Household rubbish

Pieces of pottery, wheat seeds

Large tools made from stones

Small pieces of stones and bits of bones

evidence, archaeologist, artefacts, clues.

Around the coast of north-east Ireland there are lots of lumps of flint, called **nodules**, in the white chalk cliffs and on the beaches.

When the Mesolithic people arrived in Ireland, they would have thought this a good area to live, because they used flint to make weapons and tools.

Archaeologists found lots of small pieces of broken flint at Mount Sandel, near Coleraine.

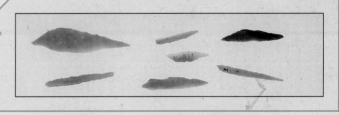

These **microliths** could have been used as knives and spear points.

The countryside contained lots of animals for them to hunt and fruits and berries for them to gather.

Talk about why the north coast of Ireland was a good place for Mesolithic hunters and gatherers.

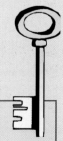

microliths, coast, nodule.

Mount Sandel

At Mount Sandel, archaeologists have found evidence of Mesolithic huts. So far, these are the oldest homes that have been found in Ireland.

Can you find Mount Sandel on this map?

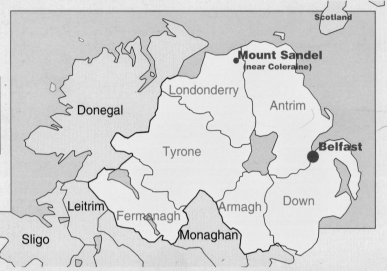

Here is the site at Mount Sandel. The poles are in the picture to show what size everything is. Each pole is 2 metres long.

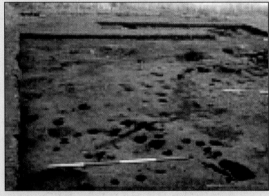

Plan of Mount Sandel hut

KEY

🔴 Dark coloured soil with bones and nut shells.

🔴 Dark coloured soil.

⚪ Dark coloured soil, burnt bones, and sharp flint.

Look at the plan and see if you can make out what they found at Mount Sandel

Can you match the places marked on the plan with the picture?

What do you think the marks on the plan show?

Mesolithic homes

From the evidence at Mount Sandel, archaeologists think that the homes of Mesolithic people may have looked like the one in this picture.

These are **reconstructions** of Mesolithic homes which have been built at the Ulster History Park near Omagh, Co Tyrone.

On the right, you can see a Mesolithic man fixing skins over the frame of his new house.

The branches are bent to make the shape of an upside down bowl. When enough branches are in place, they are covered with animal skins.

The Ulster History Park has used deer skins. Can you think of what other materials early people might have used?

Talk about why a home made out of branches and animal skins would not have lasted very long.

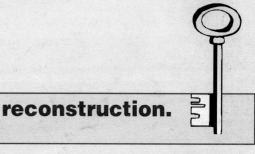
reconstruction.

Flint

The archaeologists used the clues found at Mount Sandel to describe how Mesolithic people lived.

They used flint to make spear and arrow heads.

They used bows and arrows tipped with flint to kill their prey.

They also used the flint to make tools. Sharp flat blades could be used as scrapers and knives.

weapon, tool.

Look at the picture above and see how many ways you can find flint being used as a tool or a weapon.

Flint knapping

Mesolithic people were very clever at making tools and weapons from flint.

Flint is a very hard rock which breaks into sharp pieces when it is hammered with a stone.

This is called **knapping** flint.

Look at the pictures and talk about how flint tools and weapons are made.

Write a sentence about what is happening in each picture.

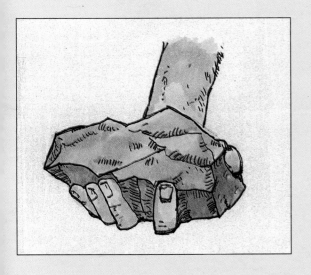

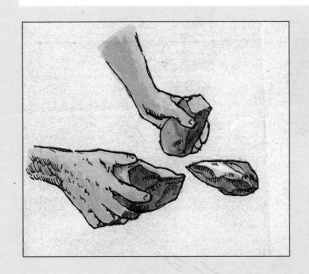

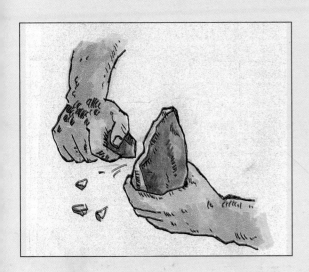

knapping.

Hunting

Imagine what it would be like to have to hunt and kill animals for your food.

You would have to be very brave and very skillful.

The drawings on this page and the next page tell the story of a hunt.

Imagine you are a young boy taking part in your first hunt.

Use these pictures to help tell your story.

Use the wordbank to help you.

Wordbank

quietly	clearing
track	forest
tracking	boar
prey	prize

Hunting fish and birds

Mesolithic men used a special spear called a harpoon to catch fish.

They were very clever because it is not easy to catch fish in this way.

They would have to know the best places to fish, where the water was not too deep or the fish too difficult to see.

The **harpoon** was shaped so that the fish was hooked and they were able to pull it out of the water.

These lifesize models of Mesolithic fishermen can be seen at the Ulster History Park, near Omagh, Co Tyrone.

Talk about why a harpoon was better for catching fish than an ordinary spear.

harpoon.

They used a bow and arrow to
shoot birds. The arrow had a flint
arrowhead tied on to it.

Gathering food from plants

It was likely that the women and children gathered the fruits and berries from the trees and bushes.

What kinds of fruits and berries do you think they are collecting in the picture?

What did they use to carry the food home?

Which berries do we pick from the hedgerows in August or September?

Where are the best places?

Some berries and plants are **poisonous** and very bad to eat.

How do you think people in early times found out which ones to avoid?

poisonous.

Making fire

We know that the first people in Ireland knew how to make fire.

They didn't have matches so what do you think they used to make fire?

Experts think they had two main methods.

Method 1

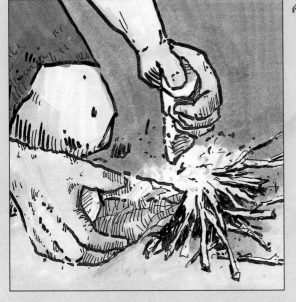

When pieces of flint are hit off each other, hot sparks are made.

Method 2

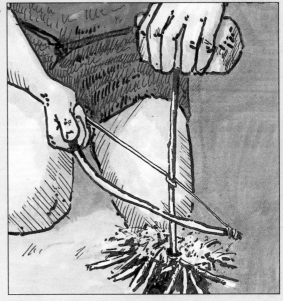

When dry sticks are rubbed together, the **friction** makes them very hot and they begin to smoke.

Talk about the two methods of making fire.

Which do you think would be easier?

Can you think of four uses for fire in early times?

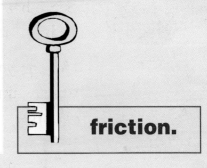

friction.

A visit to a Mesolithic camp

Imagine you could go back in time to a Mesolithic camp.

What might you see?

What kinds of things would be going on?

Use the picture on the previous page and the wordbank below to write a story about your visit to early times.

Wordbank

fire	flint	women
bow	baskets	stories
men	skins	children
sewing	fishing	cooking
scraping	boat	spit
knapping	house	clothes

The seasons

The seasons were very important to people in the past. Food was more plentiful in the spring, summer and autumn.

Look at the pictures on these two pages and talk about what they ate at different times of the year.

Spring

Summer

Autumn

Winter

Food supplies at Mount Sandel

	Spring	*Summer*	*Autumn*	*Winter*
Hazelnuts				
Other plant foods				
Wild boar				
Salmon				
Eel				
Flounder and bass				

Talk about the pictures on pages 26 and 27, and the table on page 28.

Some food could only be found at certain times.

1 What season could you gather or hunt the foods mentioned below?

Write a sentence about each one.

Salmon

Hazelnuts

Eel

Wild boar

2 In which season do you think they had the least food?

3 Which season do you think they liked best?

Facts about Mesolithic people

1   They were the first people to live in Ireland after the Ice Age.

2   They came to Ireland about 7,000 BC (about 9,000 years ago).

3   They probably came from Britain.

4   They used boats.

5   They lived by hunting animals and gathering plant foods.

6   They used flint, wood and bones to make weapons and tools.

7   At first, they used small pieces of flint.

8   Small pieces of flint are called **microliths**.

9   Later Mesolithic people made larger flint tools.

10   They could make fire.

11   Fire was used for cooking, heat and light and to scare away wild animals.

12   People roamed all over the countryside in search of food.

13   They used sticks, leaves and animal skins to make huts.

14   Apart from their flint tools, we have very few clues about their lives because wood, bone and animal skins decay.

15   Mount Sandel has given us useful clues about Mesolithic people.

16   Life in Ireland did not change very much until the arrival of the first farmers about 4,000 BC (6,000 years ago).

The first farmers

The hunting and gathering way of life had lasted for several thousand years until new people with a different lifestyle arrived in Ireland.

Archaeologists have named these people **Neolithic**, or **New Stone Age**.

They were the first people to start farming in Ireland.

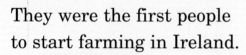

They probably hunted and gathered their food, but they also grew crops of wheat and barley and kept cattle, sheep, pigs and goats.

Except for the pigs, all of these were new to Ireland.

Neolithic, crops.

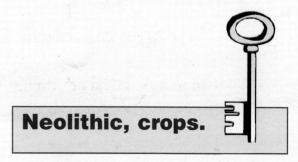

Getting animals to Ireland

Dug out canoe

Skin boat

Raft

Look at the pictures on these two pages.

Which of these do you think would have been best for bringing farm animals to Ireland?

Make a model of each of the boats shown.

Porcellanite

As well as flint, Neolithic people used another type of rock called **porcellanite**.

Porcellanite is heavier and tougher than flint. When it is shaped, polished and sharpened it could be used to make very good axes.

With these axes, the Neolithic people could cut down and split large trees.

Here is a collection of porcellanite axeheads. This collection is called the Malone Hoard, because it was found at Malone in Belfast.

Porcellanite axes could be used for other things. Here is one being used as a mattock (a digging tool) to break up the ground before planting a crop. (Ulster History Park, Omagh)

Good supplies of porcellanite were found on Rathlin Island and at Tievebulliagh, near Cushendall, Co Antrim. Archaeologists have found axe heads made from porcellanite all over Ulster, as well as in many parts of Britain and Ireland.

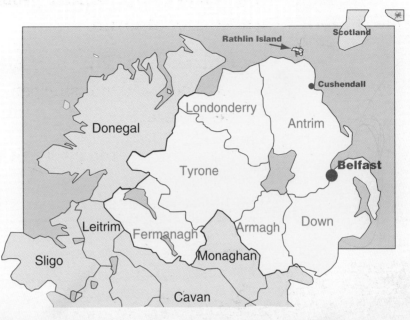

What is this man doing? Why is he doing it?

Talk about how porcellanite axe heads from Rathlin and Tievebulliagh could have got to so many parts of Britain and Ireland.

(Clue: look up 'bartering' in the glossary!)

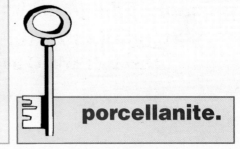

porcellanite.

Neolithic houses

When people began to farm they also began to stay longer in one place.

They still hunted and gathered fruit and berries, but now they had land and animals to look after.

They also had better tools with which to make their homes. They didn't just use branches bent over in the shape of a bowl.

The heavy axes meant they could cut down bigger trees and even make **planks**.

Here is a reconstruction of a Neolithic house. It is the Ballyglass House at the Ulster History Park near Omagh, Co Tyrone.

 What has your house got that this house hasn't got?

thatch, planks, wattle and daub.

Here you can see the framework of a Neolithic house as it is being made.

 You saw a picture of a Mesolithic house on page 15. Would a Mesolithic house or a Neolithic house take longer to make? Why?

The walls were made of wood — sometimes planks, or else using wattle and daub. Twigs were woven together and then mud was plastered into the cracks.

The roof was thatched with reeds. Bundles of reeds were fastened tightly together to keep out the rain.

The picture on page 38 shows what the inside of a Neolithic house would have looked like.

Look at the picture on page 38.

Talk about what is happening in the picture.

List the differences between the inside of this house and the inside of your house.

Use the words in the wordbank below to explain why a Neolithic house could have been a dangerous place to live in.

Wordbank

wooden walls

thatched roof

straw for bedding

open fire

children

Farming

Neolithic farmers used planks or stones to make field boundaries.

This meant they could keep their animals together and stop them from wandering away.

They could also keep them safe from wild animals, or from other people who might try to steal them.

As well as keeping animals, these first farmers in Ireland had learnt how to grow crops. Archaeologists have found evidence that they planted and harvested oats, barley and wheat.

This farmer is checking his crop to see if it is ready for harvesting.

The ripened grain was cut with a sickle.

He has to keep some grain as seed for next year's crop.

Seeds had to be collected carefully from the heads of the ripened corn.

Clearing the land

Preparing the ground

Sowing the seeds

Scaring birds

Harvesting

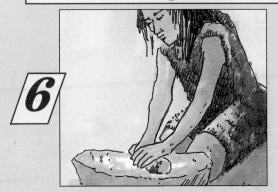

Making flour

Talk about what jobs had to be done each season.

Draw a picture for each season, and label each one.

Find a picture which shows farming in Ireland today. How has farming changed ?

Cooking

Once the wheat or barley was ripe, it was cut with a flint sickle.

To make flour for baking, the seeds were put on a broad stone, called a quern stone. Another stone was rubbed over the top and the seeds (called grain) were ground into flour.

The flour was used to make bread.

This woman is grinding corn on a quern stone to make flour.

Here is some bread baking on a hot stone which has been put on red hot embers.

quern, embers.

Pottery

Neolithic people knew how to make pots out of clay. This was a great discovery.

Pots are very useful. They can be used to store things, and carry things and can even be used to cook things in.

Small pots, filled with animal fat, make very good lamps.

Here are three pots which archaeologists have found.
They were made by Neolithic people in Ireland.

Make a list of all the things you think Neolithic people might have stored in their pots.

Think of all the pots and pans and tins and containers you have at home. What are they made out of?

Draw a picture, on one side showing your pots and on the other side of the page showing Neolithic pots.

How pots were made

Pots were made in two very simple ways.

Method 1   Just take a lump of clay and use your fingers and thumbs to squeeze it into the shape of a pot.

 Only small pots could be made in this way. Can you think why?

Method 2   Larger pots were made by rolling the clay into a thin sausage-like shape which could be coiled round to make a pot.

The coils of clay are made into a pot shape.

The clay is pressed to make the inside and outside flat.

Left: The pot is moulded into its final shape.

The pots are very soft when they are just made.

They have to be dried and then baked in a very hot oven to harden them.

Decorating pots

Some people were so proud of their pots that they decorated them with patterns.

Patterns were made by pressing sticks, seeds, cord or even fingernails into the soft clay.

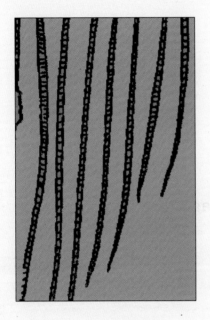

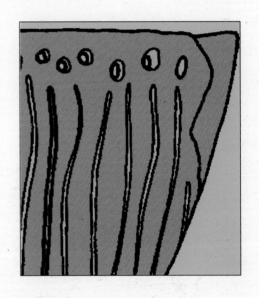

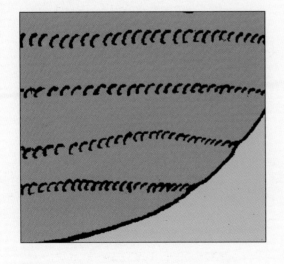

These pictures show different patterns which Neolithic people put on their pottery.

Did you know that Neolithic people didn't just store food and water in their pots?

They also stored the remains of dead people in them!

Megalithic tombs

In some parts of Ireland there are large stone mounds, which were built by Neolithic people.

Inside some of these mounds archaeologists have found pots containing human bones. This makes us think that these were places where they buried their dead.

Similar tombs or graves have been found in other parts of the world — in Spain and Portugal, France and Denmark, as well as Wales and Scotland.

These structures are called **megalithic tombs**.

There are four types of megalithic tomb:

court

dolmen

passage

wedge

Dolmens are sometimes called 'portal' tombs.

 Lithic means 'stone'. Can you guess what *mega* means?

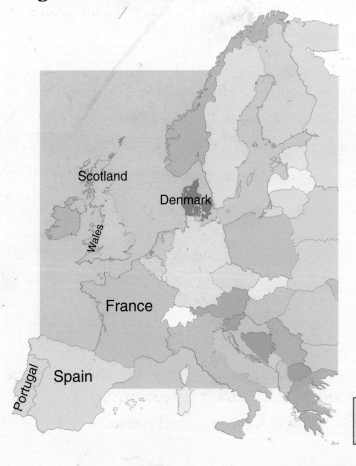

Scotland

Denmark

Wales

France

Portugal   Spain

This map shows western Europe and some of the countries where other megalithic tombs have been found.

 **megalithic, tombs.**

Court tombs

The pictures on the next three pages show three different types of tombs.

Archaeologists think that each of these would have been covered with a cairn of stones and soil.

This is what remains of a court tomb which was found at Creggandevesky in Co Tyrone.

cairn.

This is a court tomb which has been reconstructed at the Ulster History Park, near Omagh, Co Tyrone.

Dolmens

This is what remains of a dolmen or portal tomb which was found at Athanree, in Co Tyrone.

This is the dolmen which has been reconstructed at the Ulster History Park.

Wedge tombs

This is what remains of a wedge tomb which was found at Boviel, Co Londonderry.

This is the wedge tomb which has been reconstructed at the Ulster History Park.

Passage tombs

The most dramatic Megalithic tombs are the passage tombs. Stones were placed on top of one another to make a passage which led to a room or chamber.

These are some of the passage tombs which have been found at Knowth, Co Meath.

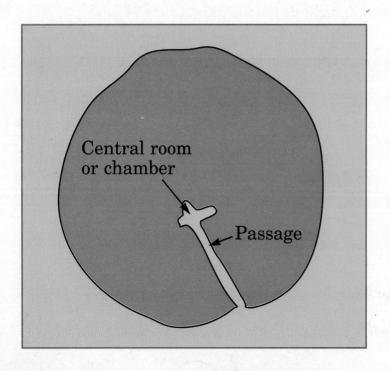

Central room or chamber

Passage

Imagine taking the top off a boiled egg. This lets you see the inside of the egg.

This diagram shows what a passage tomb would look like if you were able to take a slice through it. Just like looking down at the egg, it is as if you are looking down on a slice through the hill.

A drawing like this is called a **cross-section**.

The mystery of the Megaliths

Many experts believe that megalithic tombs were more than just places to bury the dead.

They have found clues which make them think this.

Here are some of the clues which they have found.

> They have found very few bones in each tomb.

> The tombs are usually built in places which have a very good view over the countryside.

> They are so big that they would have taken a lot of effort and people to make them.

> They all seem to have something to do with the seasons and the position of the sun in the sky.

> Many of the tombs have strange patterns carved on the large stones.

Talk about each of these clues and what they might tell us about these tombs and the people who made them.

Think about words like spring, harvest, festival, ceremony.

Newgrange

Newgrange

In Ireland, the most famous megalithic tomb is at **Newgrange**, in Co Meath, on the banks of the River Boyne.

It is a passage tomb and was built more than 4,500 years ago. Over the years it became a ruin.

In recent times archaeologists restored the tomb, using evidence they found on the site.

Newgrange

 restored.

The mystery of Newgrange

Newgrange was built so that each year, at the winter solstice, a very special thing happens.

On the shortest day, as the sun rises in the dark winter sky, its rays shine through a special opening at the entrance to the tomb.

The rays travel along the passage right to the back of the little room or chamber hidden underground.

Every year large numbers of people gather at Newgrange for this very special event.

For the lucky people waiting inside, it is a magical moment.

solstice.

This photograph was taken right inside the central chamber at Newgrange on 21st of December. You can see how the shaft of sunlight just manages to reach it.

This picture, on the left, shows the patterns which the builders of Newgrange carved on the big stone just outside the entrance.

What do you think these spiral patterns might mean?

Tombs in other lands

Ireland is not the only country where archaeologists have found large tombs.

There are many other countries in the world where early peoples built them.

Some tombs in far away lands look very different from the ones in Ireland.

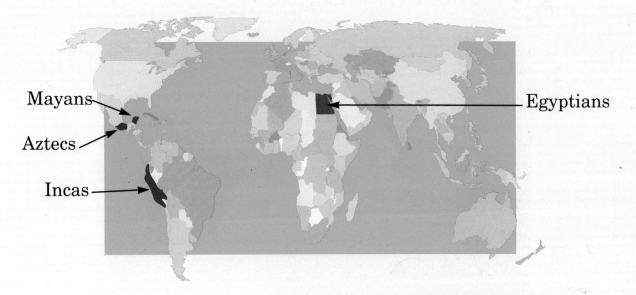

Mayans

Aztecs

Incas

Egyptians

Other people put carvings on their tombs, too.

This is a picture of part of a tomb from the Mayan civilisation in Central America.

It shows a large bird. Can you make it out?

Egypt

Many large stone tombs have been found in Egypt.

The most famous of these tombs are the **Pyramids**.

These were built for the **Pharaohs**, who were the rulers of Egypt.

Here are the Great Pyramids of Giza in the valley of the River Nile.

When a Pharaoh died, the body was **mummified** and placed in the tomb with everything which people thought the Pharaoh would need in the next world.

The picture on the right shows some of the contents of the tomb of Tutankhamun being removed after it was discovered.

Pharaoh, mummified.

Tutankhamun

Not all Pharaohs were buried in pyramids.

One of the most famous Pharaohs was Tutankhamun, the Boy King. His tomb was found in a place called The Valley of the Kings. It is dug into a hillside.

This is a picture of the gold mask that covered part of the coffin of King Tutankhamun

Here is an artist's idea of the archaeologist, Howard Carter, discovering the tomb of Tutankhamun.

Find out more about Egyptian pyramids.

Can you find out the story of how, in 1922, the archaeologist Howard Carter discovered the tomb of Tutankhamun?

Farming in Egypt

Farming had been going on in Egypt long before it had started in Ireland.

Egypt is a much warmer country than Ireland. It is much further south and did not have an Ice Age.

Ireland →

Mediterranean Sea

Egypt →

AFRICA

 Can you point to the River Nile and Cairo on this map?

 Use an atlas to find in which country the River Nile rises and which countries it flows through.

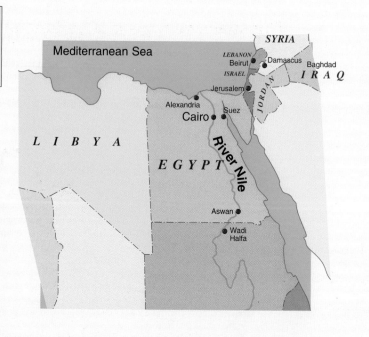

Mediterranean Sea

SYRIA

LEBANON
Beirut
Damascus
Baghdad

ISRAEL

Jerusalem

JORDAN

IRAQ

Alexandria
Suez

Cairo

LIBYA

EGYPT

River Nile

Aswan

Wadi Halfa

The Nile was very important to early Egyptian farmers.

Each year the river would flood its banks and cover the land with fresh soil and water.

This made very good farm land and the Egyptians were able to grow many crops.

Look at the pictures below and write a sentence describing what is happening in each picture.

Use your library to find out more about life in Egypt.

Facts about Neolithic people

1. They came to Ireland about 5,500 years ago.

2. They probably came from Britain, France and Spain.

3. They had boats and perhaps rafts to bring animals.

4. They brought cattle, sheep, goats and pigs.

5. They brought seeds of plants such as wheat and barley.

6. They could make fire.

7. They used fire for cooking, light, heat, firing pottery and to scare away wild animals.

8. They knew how to clear the land for farming and made fields enclosed by walls or fences.

9. They knew how to make the soil ready for sowing seeds.

10. They used other stones as well as flint for making tools — the best was porcellanite.

11. Porcellanite is found on Rathlin Island and at Tievebulliagh, near Cushendall.

12. They built houses from woven branches or planks of wood.

13. Because they were farmers, the seasons for sowing and reaping were very important.

14. They used quern stones to grind their corn.

15. They could make pots from clay.

16. We have many clues about the lives of Neolithic people because artefacts such as sickles, quern stones, axeheads and pots do not decay easily.

17. As well as homes, Neolithic people built large stone mounds or Megalithic tombs.

18. Newgrange is the largest Megalithic tomb in Ireland.

Glossary

archaeologist	a person who studies the past, sometimes by digging in the ground for evidence.
artefact	an object which has been made for a purpose.
bartering	swapping goods.
bass	a sea fish.
boar	a wild pig.
cairn	a pile of stones made by people to cover a grave or sacred place.
canoe	a simple boat made, for example, using a hollowed out tree trunk.
evidence	clues or signs left which tell people what has happened.
excavation	a dig carried out by archaeologists, who are trying to uncover evidence of the past.
flint	a hard stone which breaks into sharp pieces when it is struck. Used for tools and weapons.
flounder	a flat fish from the sea
friction	resistance when one thing rubs against another.
gatherer	a person who gathers the food they eat.

Glossary

glacier A large frozen river of ice and snow which moves very slowly. During the Ice Age much of northern Europe was covered in ice.

harpoon a barbed spear.

hunter a person who hunts for the food they eat.

Ice Age a time long ago when our part of the world was covered with ice and snow.

knapping the name given to the job of making flint tools.

megalithic *Mega* means large. *Lith* means stone. So *megalithic* means made from large stones.

Mesolithic Age *Meso* means middle. *Lith* means stone. So *Mesolithic* means Middle Stone Age.

microlith *Micro* means small. *Lith* means stone. So *microlith* means a very small piece of stone.

mummy a dead body which has been covered in oils and linen cloths. This stops the body rotting.

Neolithic Age *Neo* means new. *Lith* means stone. So *Neolithic* means New Stone Age.

nodule a piece of flint.

Pharaoh the title of the kings of ancient Egypt.

poisonous a deadly drink or food.

porcellanite a hard stone used for polished axe heads. Found on Rathlin Island and at Tievebulliagh, near Cushendall.

Glossary

post holes   marks left in the ground by the posts of a Mesolithic hut.

pots / pottery   vessels and objects made from fired clay.

pyramid   an ancient Egyptian tomb.

quern   a stone for grinding corn into flour.

raft   a boat made from logs tied together.

reconstruction   something, such as a Mesolithic hut, built to look just like the original.

restore   to build up or repair.

scraper   a stone tool for scraping animal skins or wood.

settlements   a place where people have decided to live.

sickle   a hook used for cutting grain.

spawn   when fish produce eggs, we say they are *spawning*.

tomb   grave or monument.

tool   an implement used for making things.

warrior   a person skilled in fighting.

wattle and daub   twigs or thin branches woven together which then has clay plastered onto it.

weapon   an implement used for fighting.